Richard and the Boyz the Puberty Experience

Nadine Pierre-Louis, PhD, LMFT

with Jason A. Caffey

Richard and the Boyz: The Puberty Experience
Copyright © 2019 by NADINE PIERRE-LOUIS All rights reserved.

The recommendations and information in this book are appropriate in most cases and current as of the date of publication. For more specific information about a medical condition, the author suggest that you consult a physician. Names, characters, places, and incidents are the product of the author's imagination or are used fictitiously. Any resemblance to actual persons, living or dead, events, or locales is entirely coincidental.

ISBN: 978-1-7330272-0-5 (Paperback Edition)
ISBN: 978-1-7330272-1-2 (Hardcover Edition)
ISBN: 978-1-7330272-2-9 (E-Book Edition)

Library of Congress Catalog Card Number: 2019905282

No part of his book may be reproduced in whole or in part, scanned, photocopied, recorded, distributed in any printed or electronic form, or reproduced in any manner whatsoever, or by any information storage and retrieval system now known or hereafter invented, without express written permission of the publisher, except in the case of brief quotations embodied in critical articles and reviews.

The scanning, uploading, and distribution of this book via the Internet or via any other means without permission of the publisher is illegal and punishable by law. Permission is given for individual classroom teachers to reproduce individual pages for classroom use. The reproduction of these materials for an entire school system is expressly forbidden.

Cover art copyright © 2019 by DOC N JOCK LLC
Cover art by Andre D. Burke

Books published by Doc N Jock LLC are available at special discounts for bulk purchases in the United States by corporations, institutions, and other organizations. For more information, please contact the publisher.

Visit us on the web!
www.docNjock.com

Published by Doc N Jock LLC
14886 SW 132 Avenue
Miami, Fl 33186-7615

DEDICATION

To my sons, Gene and Louis, who never failed to answer my questions no matter how cringeworthy. Thank you for always supporting your "Mom" and having my back.

TABLE OF CONTENTS

A DOCTOR'S NOTE vii
FOREWORD ix
PREFACE xi
INTRODUCTION 1
CHAPTER 1   THE "SPECIAL SAUCE" FOR GUYS
　　　　　　　　— Testosterone 3
CHAPTER 2   HAIR HERE, HAIR THERE, HAIR EVERYWHERE
　　　　　　　　— Body and facial hair 5
CHAPTER 3   WHEN WILL IT HAPPEN TO ME?
　　　　　　　　— When will my puberty start? 7
CHAPTER 4   MOM, I'LL DO MY OWN LAUNDRY!
　　　　　　　　— Wet Dreams 9
CHAPTER 5   SO, DID I PEE **AND** CUM ON MYSELF?
　　　　　　　　— The busy highway called urethra 11
CHAPTER 6   MY JUNK LEAKS IN MY SLEEP?
　　　　　　　　— What triggers ejaculation? 13
CHAPTER 7   THE RANDOM BONER
　　　　　　　　— I swear I wasn't thinkin' nothin'! 15
CHAPTER 8   MY BONER HAS NO BONE?
　　　　　　　　— The mechanics of erections 17
CHAPTER 9   WHAT GOES UP SHOULD COME DOWN
　　　　　　　　— Did your balls drop? 19

CHAPTER 10	BOUNCING BALLS — It's a thing..23
CHAPTER 11	THE BOYZ ARE LOOKING DIFFERENT — Wow, my skin is changing!................................27
CHAPTER 12	SHE LEFT ME COLD — The Pain of Blue Balls......................................29
CHAPTER 13	PIMPLES ON MY PRIVATES — and Does Color Matter?....................................31
CHAPTER 14	WHOSE PENIS IS PRETTIER? — Circumcised vs. Uncircumcised 35
CHAPTER 15	IS IT A REAL WORM? — Meet Jock-itch, his brother, Athlete's Foot, and their older sister, Ringworm 39
CHAPTER 16	DOES SIZE REALLY MATTER? — What's a Normal Penis? 43
CHAPTER 17	GROWERS AND SHOWERS — Can one penis shrink more than others?..........47
CHAPTER 18	CURVE-A-HEAD — Help! My penis is curving! 51
CHAPTER 19	JERKING OFF / JACKING OFF / WHACKING OFF / BEAT THE MEAT / CHOKE THE CHICKEN / SPANK THE MONKEY / STRANGLE THE SNAKE — The truth about masturbation..........................53
CHAPTER 20	NIP – SLIP — Am I getting boobs?..57
CHAPTER 21	"LUKE, I AM YOUR FATHER" — Oil that squeaky voice 61
CHAPTER 22	WHY IS EVERYONE IN MY BUSINESS? — Mood swings 65
CONCLUSION	69
AFTERWORD	 71
ACKNOWLEDGMENTS	73

A DOCTOR'S NOTE . . .

I have had the pleasure of Nadine's...oops...Dr. Pierre-Louis' acquaintance since middle school. This was about the time we were going through this confusing period called puberty. We briefly learned about puberty in our advanced biology class. However, the really useful information—the practical information and nuances—were not truly comprehended. Hearsay, misinformation, and old wives' tales were, and still are, prevalent today. I have been an active emergency physician for over 30 years. I have taught anatomy, endocrinology, and physiology to medical students. I have studied all aspects on this subject and consider myself an expert. I have counseled and treated many young men with issues related to this maturation process. I wholeheartedly agree with the fundamental statement presented that *"Real Men Talk."* With that said, talking is not enough—it is just a start.

Advice is only as good as the knowledge of the person who is communicating on the topic. Like the Boyz in this book, I was not given the "talk" nor did I feel comfortable at that age with this area of discussion. I was even uncomfortable when I had the talk with my two boys, as were they. This just demonstrates the need and importance of this book. Dr. Pierre-Louis not only hits the nail on the head with bridging the knowledge gap that boys and young men have regarding puberty, but she presents the information in such a way that it is easy to understand, interesting, and, quite frankly, entertaining. From a physician's perspective, the material is medically and technically accurate. The advice and recommendations are excellent and well thought out. I strongly endorse this book and its contents as a must-read for all boys of this age group. This book takes the angst of the "talk" out of the equation and imparts this knowledge in a way that will have only positive mental and physical wellbeing effects.

—MARK LIEBERMAN, M.D., F.A.C.E.P.

MARK LIEBERMAN, M.D., F.A.C.E.P. resides in South Florida. He graduated from the University of Miami School of Medicine in 1986. He was the assistant director for emergency services at Coral Springs Medical Center for 18 years. He currently works for UnitedHealthcare. In 2018 he was the first physician to receive the Sages of Clinical Practice Award.

FOREWORD

I have been blessed to work with some of the most gifted and talented athletes to ever play the game of basketball—both as a coach and as a player. While skill, talent, and a competitive spirit are common among them, these young men share the journey to the top tiers of athleticism. The route taken to get there is as individual and diverse as the players themselves. Consequently, while many arrive ready to excel at the game of basketball, some arrive emotionally unprepared. The trappings of the limelight of success become, at the very least, a distraction; at its worst, a dangerous challenge. Their lack of preparedness regarding their own physicality and responsibility off the court points to a need for the *Richard and the Boyz* series. This series helps to fill the void created when young men fail to truly understand how their bodies function and the responsibilities that come with their maturing physiology.

I first met Jason Caffey when we were both playing with the Chicago Bulls during the Championship seasons of 1995–96 and 1996–97. Jason showed a great deal of promise as an elite athlete. Unfortunately, the trappings I mentioned earlier took a toll on him down the road. I am pleased and excited to see Jason channel his experience for a positive outcome. I am impressed with his openness in sharing his life experiences to help address the misinformation perpetuated by the locker-room style communication common among males. I applaud his willingness to partner with a knowledgeable expert to help create a solid foundation of wisdom and first-hand guidance that young men can use to make sound and informed decisions as they mature. I think that *Richard and the Boyz: The Puberty Experience* is the first step in bridging the gap.

—STEVE KERR
NBA Championship Player / Head Coach – Golden State Warriors

PREFACE

As a retired NBA player, with two championship rings, having had the opportunity to play on two Chicago Bulls Championship teams (1995–96, 1996–97) alongside basketball legends like Michael Jordan, Scottie Pippen, Dennis Rodman, and Steve Kerr, it's easy to expect that my life would be a charmed one. Unfortunately, that's not the case. Once I retired from the NBA, my life took an unpleasant turn, and I made headlines for an entirely different reason. I made headlines as the father of ten children by eight women, and I was "that" guy who couldn't pay his child support. So, what does this have to do with a book about puberty? *A lot!*

When I was your age, I was focused on my size and athleticism as my ticket out of a difficult and chaotic childhood. I was the youngest of five children, and there was a ten-year gap between myself and my next youngest sister. Consequently, my brother and sisters had moved out by the time I started puberty. My parents, while they cared for me, in their own way, did not make talking easy. I grew up in an environment where verbal abuse discouraged any desire or opportunity to talk about personal issues. I was essentially on my own, both when it came to my basketball goals and when it came to understanding the changes I was going through physically and emotionally. I was taught that men didn't talk. I picked up a lot of messages about virility, manhood, sex, contraception, and disease that were misguided and produced life-long consequences. The hard reality was that I began picking up those messages from when I was your age, and the consequences followed me, as they often do, into adulthood.

Supporting this *Richard and the Boyz* series is my opportunity to do for you what was not done for me—demonstrating that *real men talk*. It is my goal, through this series, to encourage you to better understand what is happening as you become young men. It is to encourage you to ask questions and get answers. Most importantly, I want to help you find a sound basis for making decisions, which will impact you emotionally and physically for years to come.

—JASON A. CAFFEY
Retired NBA player (Champion 1995–96, 1996–97 Chicago Bulls)

INTRODUCTION

The rumbling of excitement was growing in the large crowd as they waited in line to enter the auditorium. The event was sold out for the meeting where the world-famous Dr. David Richard would be sharing important information for males.

Once the audience took their seats and the lights went down, Dr. David Richard approached the podium to a thunderous round of applause.

Raising his hands, he calmed the audience. "Thanks so much for that warm welcome, folks! I am happy to be here today to share some information that's important to us all. So, let's get started!"

The audience quieted as Dr. Richard began his presentation. "You know how they talk about guys having two brains?" he said, in his animated style. "Well, my expertise is in what we affectionately refer to as 'the other brain.' My name is Dr. David Richard. My friends call me Dr. Dick. Not too long ago, we took an informal survey of our membership and discovered there is a lot of misinformation about how and when we—the penis population—work." A chuckle rippled through the crowd.

"More importantly, we discovered that while you may learn the scientific names for things, you don't necessarily associate it with yourself. I have also heard that when we talk about ourselves, we prefer to talk about this stuff with friends instead of with parents or doctors. So, we have decided to offer an ongoing series of meetings. I will lead them and the focus will be your questions.

"My Boyz—Preeb, who is nine, and Pube, who is twelve—have agreed that we can follow them through their *puberty* experiences. We will observe their journey, and I'll comment and correct any misinformation along the way. I will also let you know the slang as well as the scientific terms involved, so you know exactly what we're talking about. I want you to remember, *real men talk!* So, feel free to ask any questions that come up along the way."

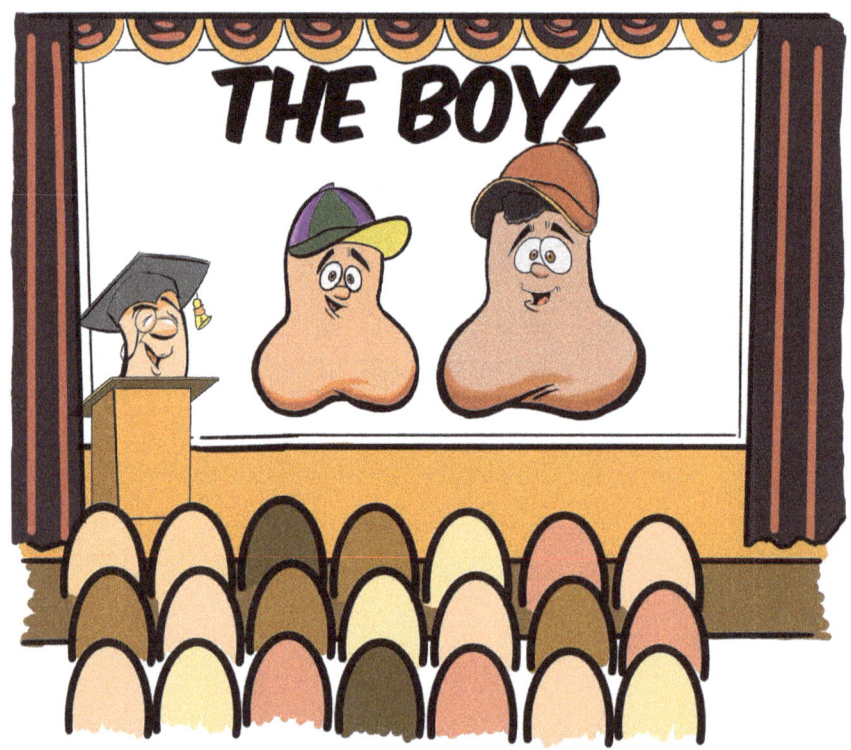

CHAPTER 1

THE "SPECIAL SAUCE" FOR GUYS — Testosterone

Preeb and Pube met up with each other after school to walk home.

"My friend Nathan told me his mom was taking a Human Growth and Development course," Pube said conversationally. "She got an assignment to write *the talk* she would give her daughter about puberty. So, Nathan asked her, 'Well, what about a *talk* for me?' And she said the professor told her to pretend she had a daughter and do the assignment."

"That sucks!" Preeb said. "Why do girls get a *talk* and we don't?"

"I guess because girls are complicated," Pube said. "And they're supposed to talk about stuff. I think guys are supposed to automatically know some stuff and figure out the rest as we go along. I do know that guys don't really talk about it. I get my best information from the locker room, listening to the older guys talk."

"That's not fair," Preeb said, clearly agitated. "I mean, I don't want the guys to think I'm a wuss or anything. I just wish someone would explain it without my having to ask."

"I'm with you, little guy!"

Dr. Richard nodded knowingly and turned to address the audience. "This is exactly what I'm talking about!" he said emphatically. "These guys should not be walking around afraid to ask questions about what is happening or going to be happening to them." Pausing for emphasis, he added, "It's important that the boys learn that *real men talk!*"

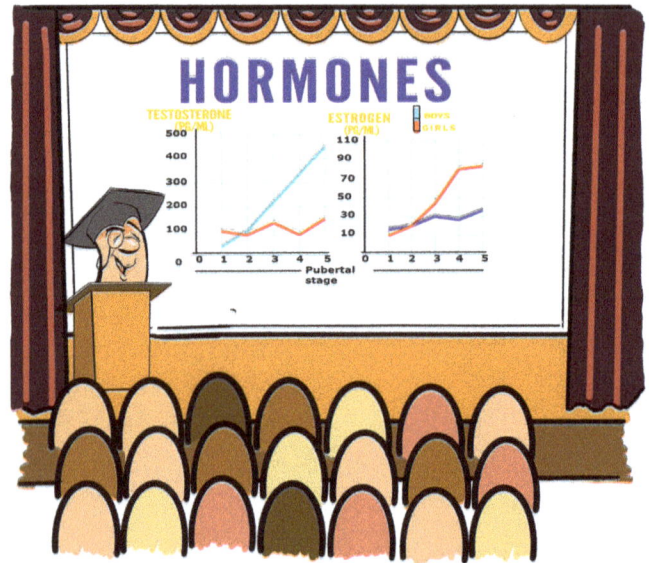

Dr. Richard continued to address his audience. "So, what *really* triggers the puberty show? In us guys, the special sauce is a chemical, a hormone called *Testosterone*. The 'other' brain sends a message to the 'boyz'—or what scientists call the *testicles*—about when to start making more testosterone; then, things start to change. Going through this change is what everyone calls *puberty*, which refers to the changes we go through to become men physically able to have kids. Girls have some testosterone, too, but not as much as guys. Their special sauce is the hormone, *Estrogen*. We've got some estrogen, too, but not as much as girls. Each of us have our own combination of hormones, so some guys will have more testosterone than others."

CHAPTER 2

HAIR HERE, HAIR THERE, HAIR EVERYWHERE — Body and facial hair

A few days later, Preeb raced to catch up with Pube on the playground. "Pube!" he said, in a hushed tone. "I've got this one random hair growing in my privates! Is that all I get? Is there something wrong with me? What's with the one hair?"

Pube laughed in response. "Dude, it's that time!"

"What time?" Preeb asked.

Pube laughed again. "Puberty, man! Hair down by your junk is the first sign. Then you'll see some under your arms. Then it'll come in on your face. Real guys can grow a full beard!"

Relieved, Preeb said, "Cool, maybe I can grow a mustache!"

"Yeah, I know a guy who had a full beard by the eighth grade!" Pube said.

Dr. Richard turned from the digital screen to face the audience. "Let me clear some things up here, guys. How much hair and where it grows is based on your family *genetics.* It has nothing to do with being a real man." He paused momentarily to let that point sink in. "If you come from a hairy family, and you start puberty later, you can continue to keep growing body hair, including on your chest or your back, into your early 20s. For almost everybody though, hair will start near your pubic bone and penis. This area is called the *groin area*. Between 11 and 15 years old, you'll notice the hair around your privates, or groin area, will start to become thicker and curlier. Once puberty starts, you'll notice hair will grow in new places between your upper legs, belly, and chest. The closer the hair comes to your groin area, the thicker, curlier, and coarser it can become."

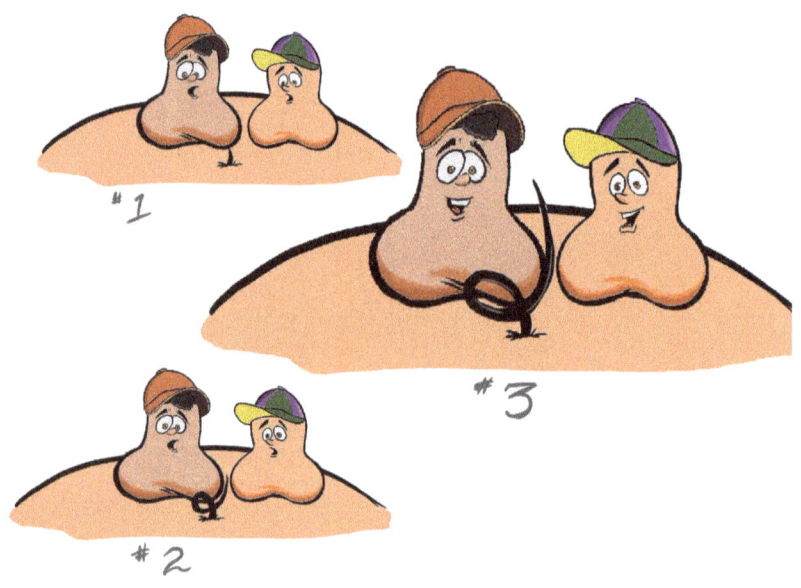

CHAPTER 3

WHEN WILL IT HAPPEN TO ME?
— When will my puberty start?

Preeb and Pube were enjoying some time hanging out at the local park. Preeb looked at Pube quizzically. "Pube, I really haven't seen any other changes since we talked. I mean other than being hungry all the time, but I don't look any fatter…How long does this puberty thing actually take? I thought I started, but nothing much seems to be happening yet."

"Well, little guy, I've heard a couple of different stories. There's a guy I knew in elementary school who said he started getting hair down there in like the fourth grade. He was 9. But there's a guy on the football team with me who refuses to change in front of anyone. He's smooth as a baby's bottom, and he's 14…. So, I can't really say when it's going to happen to you," Pube explained patiently.

Dr. Richard turned from the screen to address the crowd, nodding in agreement. "Pube is right, but there's a little bit more to the story. When you begin puberty is mostly a result of when people in your family tend to start puberty. Again, genetics. So, for example, let's say on your mom's side they started puberty around 9, but on your dad's side, they didn't start puberty until they were around 14. You can be either a late bloomer or an early bloomer, depending on which side of the family you take after. Now, about Pube's friend who's 14. If he's not showing any of the other signs of puberty—which can include things like body odor; hair around his privates or under arms, testicles, or what you all may call his balls changing; pimples; or his voice changing—his family should look into getting him examined by a doctor just to make sure everything's okay."

There was some commotion at the podium.

"If I can get everyone's attention," Dr. Richard said. "I was just handed a note from the audience… Someone wants to know, anonymously, how long can they expect their penis to keep growing once it starts."

There were cheers and laughter from the audience.

"Okay, it looks like a lot of you want to know about this one! Puberty can last about five years from when it starts, and your penis will do most of its growing both in length and width in that time. Width can take a little longer, but it can continue to grow more slowly, and your adult size should be reached by 18 to 19 years of age."

CHAPTER 4

MOM, I'LL DO MY OWN LAUNDRY! — Wet Dreams

Preeb raced to Pube's house, knocking frantically at the front door. He hurried past Pube's startled mother when she opened it, then scurried to Pube's room and burst through his bedroom door.

"Hey, Pube," he whispered. "Something really embarrassing happened to me last night. It freaked me out!"

"So, what happened, little man?" Pube asked, continuing to get ready for school.

"I woke up, and I had gone on myself!" Preeb said. "Had to hide the sheets from my mom!"

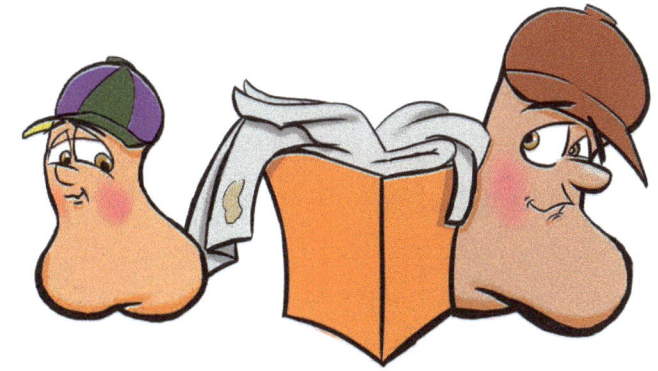

Pube stopped what he was doing and took a good look at Preeb. "What are you, about 10? The same thing happened to me at your age. Have you ever heard your friends talk about 'wet dreams?' Was it yellowish or whitish? Kinda sticky?"

Preeb thought for a moment. "Yeah, and it was whitish…."

Pube nodded knowingly. "Yeah, wet dream. Congratulations. You're becoming a man, little bro!"

Preeb flushed. "My friends talk about wet dreams, but I thought you had to be having a dirty dream. I didn't have a dirty dream! I just woke up, and there was this wet spot on the bed."

The audience became very animated while listening to this most recent exchange between Preeb and Pube. Dr. Richard banged lightly on the podium to get their attention.

"Hey, guys, let me jump in here. I know everyone here can identify with Preeb's embarrassment." He paused, waiting for the room to quiet down. "There's no cause for embarrassment. This is a normal experience in puberty. Even though most people call what we're talking about a wet dream, doctors and scientists call it *nocturnal emissions*. Remember when we were talking about *testosterone* before? Once your body starts making more *testosterone*, you're able to make sperm, the sperm combines with liquid, and together it's called *semen*. When you talk about it, you probably call it cum. It looks like a whitish liquid. The *sperm* is produced in the *testicles,* or what you refer to as your balls, which are covered by what science refers to as your *scrotum*. Being able to make *sperm* is what allows you to be able to make babies or *reproduce*. It is possible, even if you didn't have a sex dream. Friction from contact with your bedding or something else can frequently be enough to trigger a wet dream. Although, it's also possible to have a sex dream and not remember."

CHAPTER 5

SO, DID I PEE AND CUM ON MYSELF?
— The busy highway called urethra

"Dude," said Preeb, hoping to draw Pube's attention from the comic he was reading. "Remember a couple of days ago, when we were talking about that accident? The one I had the other night?" He paused to ensure he had Pube's complete attention. "I heard what you said, but I'm still a little confused. Pee and semen are coming out from the same place?"

Pube stopped to think for a moment. "Uhh, I'm not really sure about that one," he said, sounding befuddled. "I know they come out the same hole but not at the same time—but I never really thought about why not...." His voice trailed off.

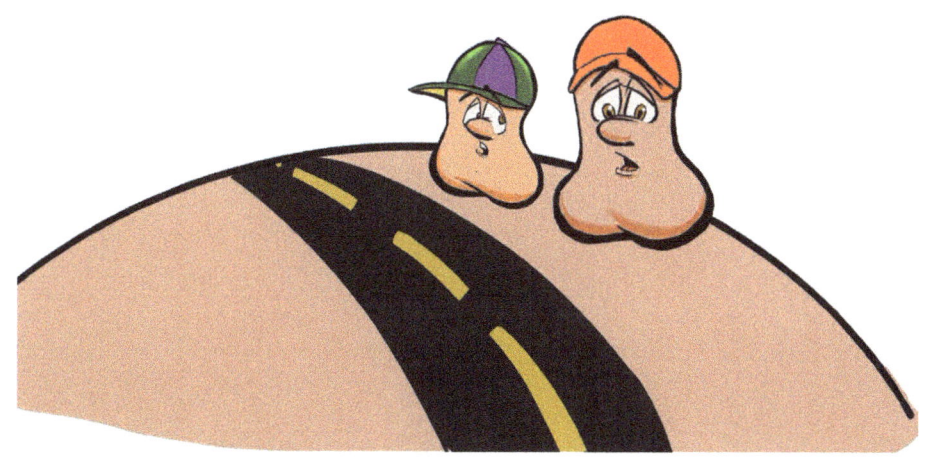

Dr. Richard addressed the audience. "Let me help the Boyz out on this one. The urethra is the tube in the penis that carries both urine and semen, so they *do* both come out of the same opening at the end of the penis. When a male releases sperm, this is called *ejaculation*. The muscles tighten to keep the urine in his bladder, so that they *don't* travel through the urethra at the same time."

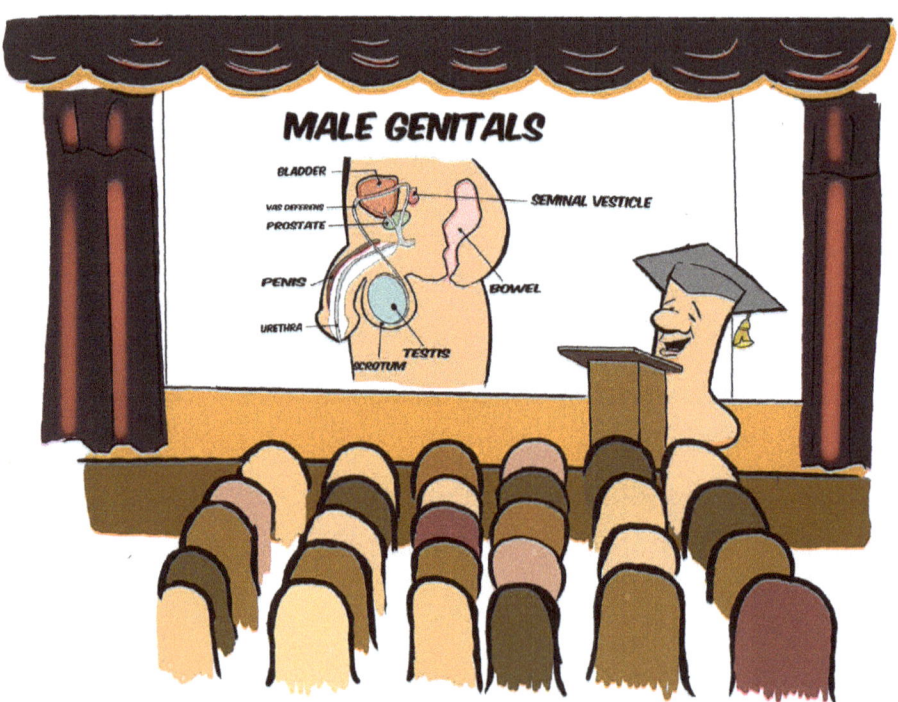

CHAPTER 6

MY JUNK LEAKS IN MY SLEEP?
— What triggers ejaculation?

A few hours later, Preeb once again picked up the discussion, as if there was never a break. He looked at Pube and asked, "So if I don't pee in my sleep, why do I cum in my sleep?"

Pube lifted his head from his comic, thought for a minute, and responded. "Damn, that's a good one.... If I had to guess, you get the boner in your sleep from a dream, and you finish the dream so out it comes...."

Dr. Richard interjected enthusiastically. "What Pube is guessing is not far off. It just doesn't tell the whole story." Turning to the IT person, Dr. Richard said, "Can you put our penis slide back up? Thanks." With his attention once again on the audience, Dr. Richard continued.

"Okay, what we are talking about is how does a penis go from erection to ejaculation, or as others may refer to it, when a penis goes from a boner or a woody, to bustin' a nut. This part is a little technical, so follow the highlighted areas of the slide. Muscles in the *epididymis, vas deferens, seminal vesicles,* and around the *prostate gland* tighten and push the semen into the urethra, and then it gushes out. The gushing portion is scientifically called *ejaculation* but is more commonly referred to as 'blowing your load,' 'shooting your load,' 'cuming,' 'busting your wad,' or, as mentioned before, 'bustin' a nut.' Along with ejaculation, you usually experience extreme pleasure. This experience is called an *orgasm*. This experience is what you may hear referred to as '*climax*.'

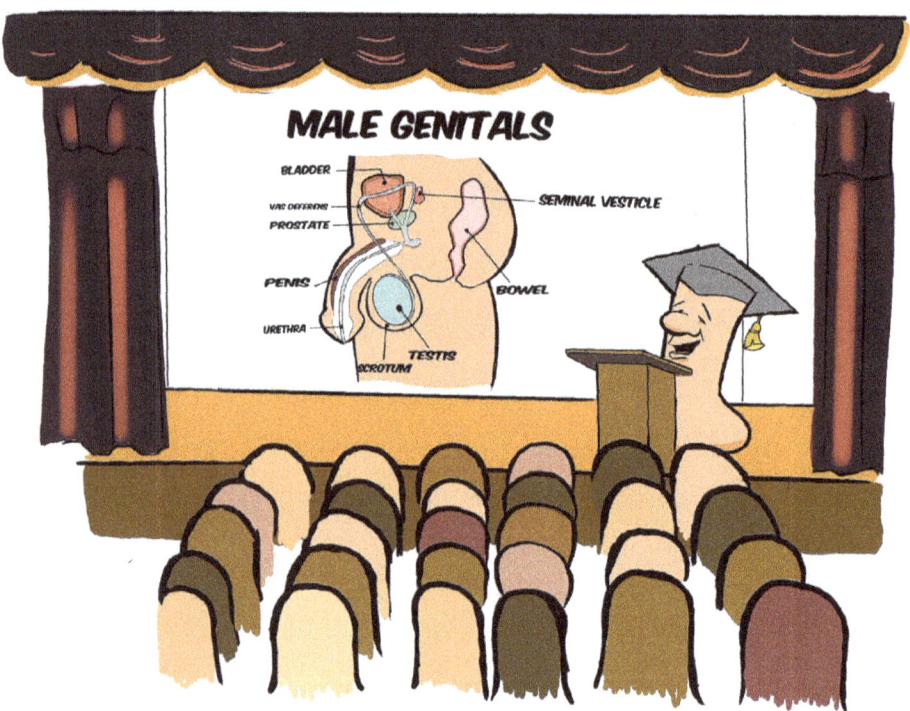

"Just because you have an erection does not mean you have to ejaculate. The blood flow can leave the penis slowly and return to the body, the erection will slowly go away, and your penis will become soft again. You've been having erections all your life, but *ejaculation* is one of the changes that comes with puberty."

CHAPTER 7

THE RANDOM BONER — I swear I wasn't thinkin' nothin'!

Preeb was sitting in his fourth grade classroom when his phone began to vibrate on his desk. Looking down, he saw a text from Pube.

"Preeb, you gotta help me! Bring me your sweater or something. I'm in class, and I've got this unbelievable boner. I swear I wasn't thinkin' nothin'! That fine girl I told you about is coming in any second. This is embarrassing. Hurry up!"

Preeb hurriedly looked around to see whether anyone could read his cellphone. Skeptical, he messaged back, "If you weren't thinkin' nothin', why'd it happen?"

Pube's response quickly lit up the phone screen. "Just SHUT UP and bring me a sweater or something. Oh damn, never mind. She just walked in. I'm sitting with my backpack on my lap. No matter what, I CAN'T look at that girl! She's saying hi. I CAN'T LOOK, TALK, OR THINK ABOUT THAT GIRL! I'm

15

pretending I didn't hear her. I have to keep my backpack on my lap until the boner goes down."

Preeb typed back quickly, looking up as his teacher entered the classroom. "Good luck. I've got to go. Class is starting."

The auditorium erupted in conversation following their viewing of Preeb and Pube's exchange. Dr. Richard moved back to the podium.

"I know all of you older guys remember this experience and can sympathize. It's seriously embarrassing. We feel for Pube. Unfortunately, most of us didn't have anyone tell us this could happen—until it does. Now, here's what is actually going on." He paused as the rumbling died down.

"What the Boyz are calling a boner, and some of you may call 'a hard on,' is actually a *spontaneous erection*. And a couple of years into puberty, you can get an erection or boner anytime, doing anything. It's kind of nature's random plumbing check. You don't have to be excited or thinking about sex. You can be awake or asleep. Even though you've been having erections all your life, usually in the mornings when you have a full bladder, what is happening now is different." Dr. Richard looked out at the audience before continuing.

"These spontaneous erections are a result of the increased production of testosterone, the special sauce we talked about earlier. During puberty, your hormone levels fluctuate. The best comparison I can use is when we turn on a faucet. We keep adjusting the hot and cold levels until we get it right. Your body is going through something similar, and so production of your hormone levels is going through its own plumbing checks until it levels off. As you get older, *spontaneous erections* will happen less and less."

CHAPTER 8

MY BONER HAS NO BONE?
— The mechanics of erections

Preeb and Pube were chillin' out in the yard.

"Pube," Preeb said, tentatively, "don't judge, okay?"

Pube laughed. "No promises, little guy, but I'll try."

"So, when I get a boner, why does it get hard?" Preeb asked. "Like is there some kind of bone down there or what?"

Pube took a deep breath, stalling as he struggled for a response. "You've got a lot of questions I really haven't thought of before. I know that dicks fill up and stuff, but I never gave much thought about the mechanics of what makes me hard, other than 'getting friendly.' I know a friend of mine said it was cartilage, like the soft part of a chicken bone, or like in the tip of your nose...." His voice trailed off, sounding unsure.

Dr. Richard stepped back to the podium, interrupting the live stream of the Boyz.

"Okay, guys," he said, looking out at the audience. "I have got to interrupt here before we wander too far down this rabbit hole." He took a breath before continuing. "Let me first state this in a way I know everyone will understand. There is no bone or cartilage in your penis. Period." He paused to ensure his words were heard and understood. "An *erection,* or as you may refer to it, a boner, woody, or stiffy, is all about muscles, tissue, and blood flow. When the penis is not erect—what you may call a limp dick, or what the professionals call *flaccid*—small amounts of blood are traveling in and out of the penis. When you have an erection, the muscles that control the blood into the penis open wide so that more blood is pumped in, and some other muscles tighten and keep the extra blood from leaving. The tissue fills up, and the result is your penis becomes stiff—or to be clear, your penis gets hard and stands up and away from your body.

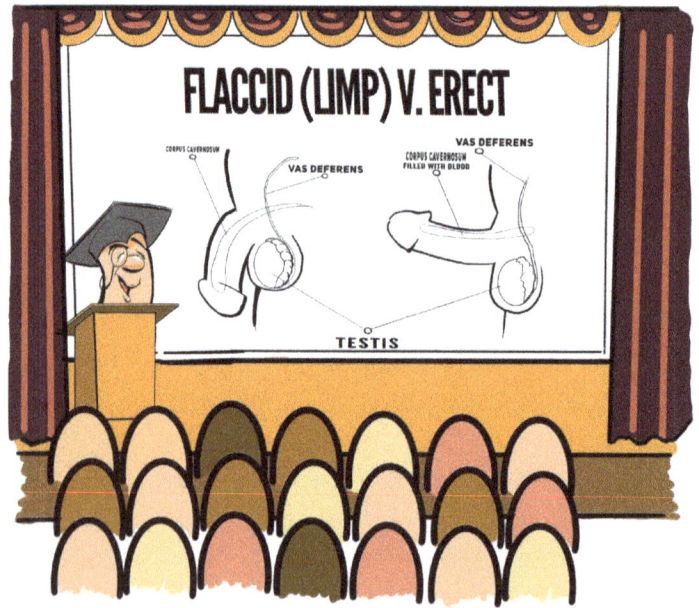

"When the erection is over, the muscles relax and allow the blood to flow back into the body from the penis. The penis becomes soft once again, hence the limp dick."

CHAPTER 9

WHAT GOES UP SHOULD COME DOWN — Did your balls drop?

The digital screen in the auditorium lit up once again with the images of Preeb and Pube. This time, they were near the school playground, talking.

Preeb looked over at his friend and said, "Hey, Pube, I heard some guys talking about 'balls dropping.' I didn't get it and didn't want to ask. Do you know what they're talking about?"

Pube paused a moment before answering. "It's not what you think...." He hesitated. "If I tell you something, you have to promise not to tell anyone, swear?" He looked at Preeb expectantly.

Preeb, curious, immediately answered, "Okay, I swear."

Pube looked around to make sure no one was listening. "I kept hearing the guys talking about their balls dropping, too, so I kept checking." He paused, glancing down at himself. "I mean, I got one that hangs lower than the other, but they never really dropped, at least not the way I expected." After another brief pause, he continued. "You know how it's just me and my mom? So, I couldn't ask her. That would be toooooo embarrassing."

Pube fell silent, trying to decide whether he should continue. After a moment, he took a deep breath and started talking in a low tone. "Last month, I went on a message board on the Internet to see if I could find out when it was supposed to happen, especially since I'm 12. I was scared something was wrong with me. It turns out that 'did your balls drop?' is code for 'can I shoot my wad?'" Pube fell silent again.

Preeb continued to look at Pube expectantly, but his friend said nothing further. After a while, Preeb sheepishly looked at him and said, "I know you think I understand what you just said, but I don't...."

Dr. Richard paused the image on the screen. "Okay, listen up! There's a lot to talk about in this exchange. First off, guys, the Internet is great for getting information quickly and anonymously, but just because you see something on the Internet doesn't mean it's accurate. You have to be careful that the websites you're posting your questions on are reliable and safe. On some message boards, forums,  and blogs, the answers are coming from other people just like you, so they are probably not experts. The information they share may not be accurate. If you would rather search on the Internet because you're not comfortable talking to a parent or waiting until you see your doctor, then make sure it's a site supported by an expert, like a hospital or university. They have licenses, which they risk if they don't give the public good information.

"It's always a good policy to double check what you think you understand with your doctor at your next checkup. Once you start puberty, the doctor will ask your parent to step out for part of your exam, so it's a good time to ask any questions that may make you feel embarrassed. I doubt you are going to ask a question the doctor hasn't heard before, so go ahead and take the opportunity to get good information." Dr. Richard paused for a moment before continuing.

"Now, let's tackle balls dropping," he stated good-naturedly. "This one, believe it or not, is a popular misconception." He looked directly at his audience. "I'm willing to bet there are a couple of you out there today who are still confused about this one." He noticed affirmative nods from the audience. "Lots of guys walk around expecting their balls to actually drop in puberty. This is because when they hear the phrase, they are thinking about their testicles and can be too embarrassed to ask. The  reality is that the actual dropping of the testicles into place normally occurs in infancy. I know some of you are surprised to hear that," he said, laughing. "On occasion, once the testicle has *descended,* or dropped, there is a muscle called the *cremaster,* which can pull the testicle back into the *scrotum,* or what you may call the ball sac. This is normal."

Dr. Richard reached for a sip of water before he continued. "In common everyday discussion, when guys ask if your balls have dropped, they want to know whether you're making *sperm* yet. The way you know whether you're making *sperm* is if you have *ejaculated,* or as Preeb put it, if he could 'shoot his wad.'"

CHAPTER 10

BOUNCING BALLS — It's a thing....

The next day, the audience once again shuffled into the auditorium to take their seats as the images of Preeb and Pube come up on the screen. The Boyz were at the basketball courts, conversing on the sidelines. Preeb leaned over and said, "Pube, a guy was telling a story the other day about why he won't go swimming anymore. He said the water made his balls shrivel back into his body. Can that happen for real?"

Pube laughed dismissively. "Dude, your friend needs to get a grip. It's just temporary. His nads will go back to normal. Swimming doesn't hurt anything!"

Smiling, Dr. Richard turned to the audience. "Okay, what guys lovingly refer to as 'their boyz,' or 'nads,' is their *testicles*. The *testicles* produce sperm. Now, when guys talk, they generally use the word 'balls' or 'nuts' to refer to their *testicles*. With regard to shriveling, guys are talking about what they feel and not what they see. What they see is the 'sac' that hangs behind their penis. The 'sac,' in scientific terms, called the *scrotum*, is the soft sac that covers and holds the testicles. It's important to understand the distinction, because the *scrotum* holds more than just the *testicles,* which produce *sperm*. It also holds the *epididymis* that houses the *sperm* on its way to the *vas deferens*, which delivers the sperm to the *urethra*. The *testicles*, in puberty, will grow to the size of a walnut or small ball, which is how they earned the nicknames 'nuts' and 'balls.' Unfortunately, when guys talk, they use the same words when talking about the *testicles* as when they talk about the *scrotum*. The easiest way to know which one they really mean is to remember the following: If they're talking about what their balls look like, they're talk-

ing about the *scrotum*. If they're talking about how their nuts feel, they're talking about their *testicles*. For example, 'My balls are different sizes.' If they're talking about an experience, like getting kicked in the nuts, they're talking about everything in the *scrotum*."

Dr. Richard paused at this point, then said, "I realize this is a lot of information, but if you spend a minute looking at the chart and following the path the *sperm* takes, from start to finish, you'll see it is not as complicated as it sounds."

Dr. Richard gave everyone a moment to examine the slide entitled, *Male Genitals.*

As the room quieted down, Dr. Richard continued. "Now to Preeb's bouncing balls story. To produce sperm, the surrounding temperature needs to be a little cooler than the normal body temperature of 98.6 degrees Fahrenheit." He gave the room a moment to digest this information. "In fact, the optimal temperature is about 95 degrees Fahrenheit. To remain cooler is why the *testicles* hang away from the body. Remember earlier we were talking about the *cremaster* muscle?" Dr. Richard quickly looked around the room to make sure everyone was following before he continued. "Well, the primary job of the cremaster muscle is to help regulate the temperature of the *testicles.* It pulls them closer to the body to access body heat when in a cold environment, and it releases the testicles when the environment is warm. The *cremaster* muscle also has a second job. When you get anxious and your fight or flight response is triggered, and you need to fight or run, the cremaster muscle will pull the *testis* closer to the body to protect them."

Dr. Richard let out a laugh. "An interesting but unrelated fact. There is a *cremasteric reflex*—a light stroke or poke along the inside upper thigh will trigger the muscle to pull the testis into the body on that side only. Just a fun fact I thought I'd share," he stated, grinning from ear to ear.

CHAPTER 11

THE BOYZ ARE LOOKING DIFFERENT
— Wow, my skin is changing!

Pube stared at himself pensively in his bedroom mirror. "I don't get it. The skin feels different down there…rougher. When I look, it looks like it's getting darker. I can't ask Preeb about it. He's younger than me. And I can't ask any of the guys on the team because they'll think I'm weird."

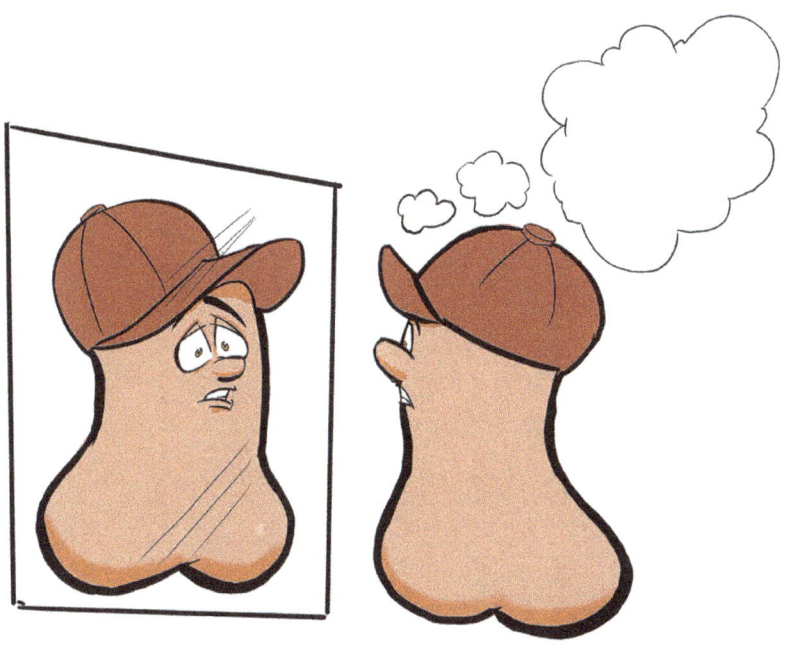

Dr. Richard paused the image of Pube and turned to his audience. "What our friend Pube is noticing is something we all go through. There are a couple of different changes that you will notice to your balls, or *scrotum*, during puberty. You will notice that they are getting bigger than they were. This is in preparation for the manufacture and delivery of *sperm*. Next, you might notice one side hanging lower than the other. When you feel your *scrotum*, you can feel that one testicle hangs higher than the other. This is normal. If your balls or testicles hung evenly, then it would be easier for your *testicles* to get damaged because it would be easier for them to get smushed together. In a 'nut' shell…" Dr. Richard paused to make sure everyone got the joke. "You know, balls, nuts…"

The audience laughed and some rolled their eyes.

"Okay, bad joke, tough crowd," Dr. Richard said. "Anyway, as I was saying, there's just not enough room for the *testis* to safely hang next to each other. You may have noticed that I used the word *testis* instead of

testicles. I am not trying to confuse you. Either word is scientifically appropriate to refer to your balls." He allowed this information to sink in. "Something else you will notice is that the skin around your balls, or *scrotum*, will get darker, thinner, and rougher. This is what our friend Pube is experiencing. Your skin is getting darker because of the increased production of male hormones."

CHAPTER 12

SHE LEFT ME COLD — The Pain of Blue Balls

Pube looked down at his cellphone. The text message read, "Beware of teases. They'll give you blue balls!"

Preeb was trying to peek at the phone from behind him.

"Watch out, little man. This is for us older guys. You're not ready for this!" Pube stated, as he pulled away from Preeb.

"Not true!" Pube said in a whiny voice. "I've heard you and your friends talking about blue balls before! Do your balls really turn blue? Has that happened to you?"

Dr. Richard paused the images on the screen before speaking. "Okay, guys, like the other topics we've discussed, blue balls also has a fancy name. It's called *epididymal hypertension,* or EH for short. Don't worry about memorizing the word unless you plan on competing on *Jeopardy*." He paused as he realized this joke went right over their heads. "You guys may be too young a crowd to watch *Jeopardy*," he said, shaking his head.

"Now, this is a topic with some serious misinformation floating out there," Dr. Richard said. "Blue balls, or *EH,* has nothing to do with how a girl behaves. The guy who sent Pube the text totally got it wrong! When guys talk about blue balls, they are discussing the pain that can sometimes accompany an *erection* that lasts a while without *ejaculation*.

"The blue part comes from the fact that in some cases your *scrotum,* or 'sac,' can look bluish. The bluish color is from the increased unrelieved blood flow and blood pressure to the area that normally accompanies an *erection*. The pain or ache, which in some cases accompanies blue balls, or *EH,* is temporary and goes away on its own.

"*Masturbation* is also an option for relieving *EH*," he said. "We will go into *masturbation* in greater detail later in the series. Having blue balls will not harm your *testicles*. Now, jumping back to Pube's friend—if you are easily stimulated, you are more likely to experience EH."

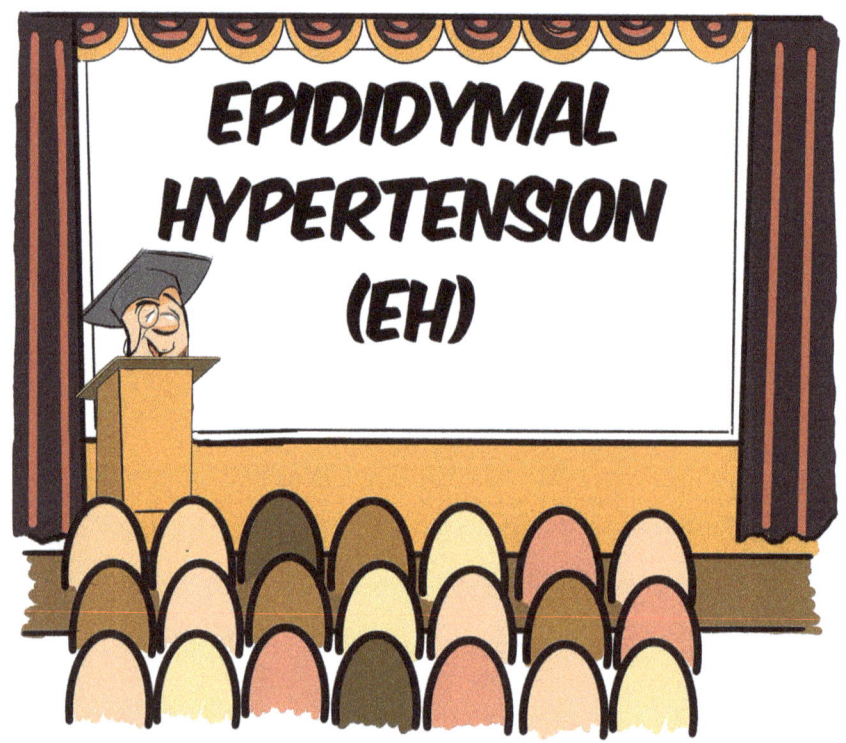

CHAPTER 13

PIMPLES ON MY PRIVATES — and Does Color Matter?

Pube ran up to Preeb in a panic. "I don't know what to do! You can't say a word to anybody! You have to swear!" Without waiting for a response, Pube continued. "I think I got an STI! But how is that possible? I haven't done anything yet! I might have played with myself a little…I can't tell my parents. They'll kill me!" Pube stopped talking and finally took a breath.

"What makes you think you have an STI?" Preeb asked, concerned for his friend.

"I've got a bump on my balls!" Pube responded anxiously. "I've heard some of the older guys talking about bumps on your privates is a symptom of an STI. What am I going to do? Preeb, you can't tell anyone. Swear!" he said, clearly agitated.

Dr. Richard immediately interrupted. "I need to stop you guys right now," he said in a concerned tone. "If you ever think something is wrong with your privates, it's important that you find out right away since the longer a *Sexually Transmitted Infection*, or STI, goes untreated, the greater the risk." He paused for a moment, then added, "That said, in this particular case, it is highly unlikely that Pube has an STI. As he mentioned, he hasn't had any physical contact with anyone, so it is highly unlikely. What he is probably experiencing is a pimple, which is not uncommon, especially in active boys.

"Sweat and dead skin cells are the primary cause of pimples on the scrotum and will usually go away without treatment—the same as pimples on your face and other parts of your body. To be on the safe side, let's talk about pimples in a little more detail. Hopefully, you aren't too squeamish.

"First, there are your *blackheads*, which are caused by trapped oil clogging your pores. The top will appear black when the air hits it.

"Next, there are your *whiteheads,* which are like the blackheads, except the pore is closed so it appears white.

There are *pustules* that are white in the center, which is caused by the accumulation of pus. These are the pimples that, when they're on your face, no one can resist the temptation to pop them.

"There are *papules*, which appear red with no head. They are solid and may feel sore when touched. Chickenpox is an example of papules.

"Finally, there are *nodules*, which are firm papules that develop below the skin, like a cyst. I also want to mention that you can get a heat rash on your scrotum as well, which will appear as small red bumps that may be itchy or prickly."

Dr. Richard paused to let this sink in before continuing. "Things that can cause pimples on your privates include *tight-fitting clothes, humidity, excessive sweating, shaving, poor hygiene,* and *oily skin.*"

Dr. Richard briefly glanced around the room, noting some in the audience scribbling notes. "I also want you to know that you can get a pimple on your penis the same way you can get them on your *scrotum*," he said. "Since we are discussing growths on your penis, I need to discuss a specific type of *papule,* which can grow on your penis. It is known as *pink penile papules,* or *PPP*. They can grow around the head of the penis in a single or double row. They are small, non-cancerous growths that can look pink, white, yellow, and occasionally translucent. They aren't harmful, and they are not contagious. They are not race specific or limited to a geographic area. It does appear to have been reported to occur more among black males and uncircumcised males."

Looking out at the room, Dr. Richard added, "PPP is not a sexually transmitted infection or STI. It can appear on children who are not sexually active. Since PPP can look like an STI, it is best to have the growths checked—especially if they appear after becoming active. If you have PPP, you may be tempted to try to pop them like a pimple to get rid of them. THIS IS NOT A GOOD IDEA," Dr. Richard said. "You can create an open wound on your penis. If you notice you have them, you may feel embarrassed, but don't be ashamed to tell your parents to take you to the doctor so you can learn more. PPP isn't harmful, and you didn't do anything to get them!" He stressed this last point emphatically.

"Now, some of you may think I dismissed Pube's concern too quickly." He paused, looking intently at the audience. "I just want you to be informed to avoid unnecessary panic. So, when should you see a doctor about pimples on your privates? One, if you **keep** getting pimples on your scrotum despite exercising good hygiene or cleaning practices; two, if your pimples appear in clusters or grouped together; three, if they look like a rash; and four, if you're not sure and your pimples are red—as red can indicate an irritation or infection.

"In conclusion," Dr. Richard said, "when in doubt, get checked by a medical professional."

CHAPTER 14

WHOSE PENIS IS PRETTIER? —
Circumcised vs. Uncircumcised

Preeb and Pube gathered their belongings as they prepared to leave the girls' volleyball game.

"Yo, Preeb," Pube said, glancing around to make sure no one was within earshot. "Something's been bothering me." He paused once again, glancing around to make sure they were alone before continuing. "You're the only one I can talk to about this who won't take it the wrong way…. I was in the shower after our first practice yesterday."

Preeb was pleased that Pube would trust him, since he was younger, but he was also a little fearful of what might be said next. "What happened?" he asked.

"Nothing really happened…" Pube paused again, and Preeb let out a breath that he didn't realize he was holding.

"It wasn't like I was looking around or anything, but I kinda noticed that one of the guys has something like a growth hanging at the end of his junk! I didn't want to look like I was staring or anything, so I looked away quick. I wonder if there's something wrong with him?"

Dr. Richard paused the projector screen and brought up a new slide. "This one is a sensitive topic for a lot of guys," he said. "Based on his comments, Pube seems to have a circumcised penis, and the teammate who caught his attention appears to have an uncircumcised penis. At Preeb's age, this is not something boys are frequently aware of, but they should be, as penis hygiene—especially going into puberty—is a little different depending on whether you are circumcised or uncircumcised."

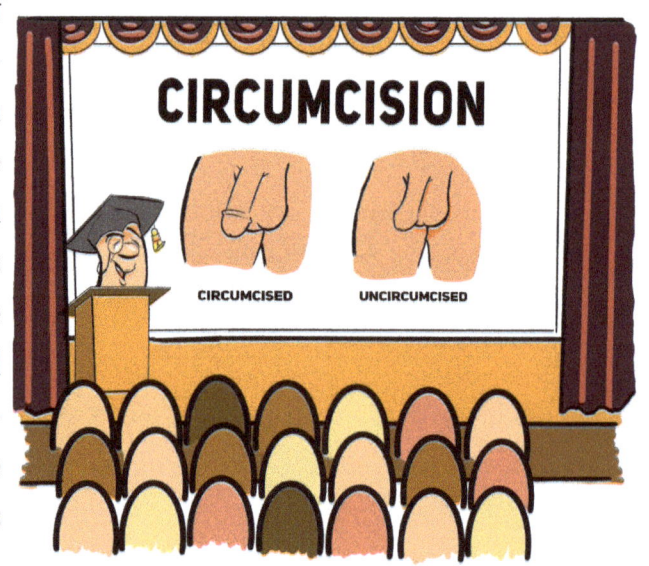

Dr. Richard took note of the confused faces in the audience. "Let's deal first with describing circumcision," he said. "Boys are born with a layer of skin, which covers the head of the penis. The head of the penis is referred to as the *glans*. In circumcision, that skin, called the foreskin, is removed. This leaves the *glans* exposed. While it can be done later, parents normally will have made a decision to have their child circumcised, or not, sometime between birth and their first year. This decision can be based on any number of reasons, including religion and culture."

Dr. Richard paused to make sure the audience was following him. Satisfied that they were grasping what he was saying, he went on, "Which is better? There's no clear answer to that question. What I want to focus on is the physical aspects of the difference between being circumcised and uncircumcised. It is important for boys, during puberty, to maintain proper hygiene and clean and dry their penis as part of their daily routine. Boys who are uncircumcised need to make sure they take the extra step of pulling back the foreskin from the head, or *glans,* of the penis to ensure they properly clean the area. Pulling back the foreskin is called *retracting*. If you don't clean under the foreskin, dead skin cells and other residue can collect between the glans and the foreskin, resembling a cheesy-like substance called *smegma. Smegma* can give off an unpleasant smell. Consequently, keeping the head of the penis under the foreskin clean is important."

Dr. Richard paused before adding, "In addition, pulling the foreskin back avoids the development of a condition called *phimosis. Phimosis* is when the foreskin gets stuck to the head of the penis, and the penis gets sore and swollen. If this occurs and there's pain and trouble urinating, it's best to go see your doctor," he said. "Now don't assume if you can't pull your foreskin back that something is wrong. It's not unusual with young boys for the foreskin to not pull or *retract* all the way back from the head of the penis. Don't force it. Over time, the foreskin will loosen, and by 17, most guys can pull the foreskin all the way back."

Concluding, Dr. Richard stated, "The bottom line with circumcised penises and uncircumcised penises is that it's important to keep the head clean, especially once puberty begins."

CHAPTER 15

IS IT A REAL WORM? —
Meet Jock-itch, his brother, Athlete's Foot, and their older sister, Ringworm

Preeb caught up with Pube as he exited the locker-room.

"I felt kind of bad for this guy at practice today," Pube said. "The guys were giving him a hard time, calling him nasty, because he has some kind of rash near his nads. Poor guy was itching like crazy. I don't know what they were talking about, but I wasn't going to shower with him because I didn't want to get whatever he's got."

Preeb looked at him quizzically. "Can you get it from just being around him?"

Pube shrugged. "I don't really know, but the guys made it sound really gross, so I'm just going to stay away from him for a while to be on the safe side."

Dr. Richard paused the projector and turned to the audience. "If the rash the guys are talking about looks like a half-moon near the young man's groin, it sounds like the guys are talking about *Jock-itch,* or *tinea cruris*. Don't worry about learning the fancy name. Even the doctors call it Jock-itch," he said. "If it's Jock-itch, it'll look like a half circle, reddish or scaly, right around the groin."

Dr. Richard stopped briefly. "Now before I go any further, I need to clear up a little geography," he said, smiling. "When we talk about a guy getting kicked in the *groin,* or nuts, what we really mean is that he got kicked in the *scrotum*. However," he said, "the groin technically is the triangle area that is just below the abdomen or stomach but above the thighs. This is important because you don't usually get Jock-itch on your penis or scrotum." Dr. Richard stopped again to make sure the audience was following him.

"So, let's talk about Jock-itch. Jock-itch is a type of skin fungus that likes to grow in moist areas of the body. It's called Jock-itch because it likes to grow in warm, moist, sweaty areas, which is easy to find on an athlete's body. Jock-itch is part of a family of fungus known as *tinea,* which is the same family of fungus that gives you Athlete's Foot and Ringworm. In fact, Jock-itch is sometimes referred to as Ringworm of the groin. Because of this fungal relationship, Jock-itch is contagious and can also be spread to other parts of your body." Dr. Richard looked out at the audience to make sure he had everyone's attention.

"If you have Jock-itch, it's possible to give yourself Athlete's Foot if your foot touched the crotch area of your underwear when you're getting dressed. So, how do you avoid getting Jock-itch?" he asked the audience. Not waiting for a response, he said, "Keep your skin clean and dry, especially your upper thighs and groin area. Make sure to remove as much moisture as possible. Select quick-drying athletic clothes, like dri-fit materials. Change underwear daily and after exercising. Avoid tight clothes, especially underwear and jockstraps. Don't reuse athletic clothes without washing them first. Don't share towels. Don't share gym clothes if you're not sure whether they've been washed. Jock-itch can survive on hard surfaces, so wipe gym equipment before using. Finally, wear sandals in public showers and pool-side. Remember, Jock-itch and Athlete's Foot are related."

CHAPTER 16

DOES SIZE REALLY MATTER? —
What's a Normal Penis?

Pube walked up to Preeb as he exited the Boy's Room at school.

"Pube, you're never going to guess what I saw when I was in there." He paused expectantly.

"What did you see?" Pube asked, curious.

"I was reading the bathroom wall at school, and it said that Peter's junk is so small he has to pee sitting down." Preeb looked at Pube before continuing. "My dad's short. I don't want anybody making fun of me like that! What do I do?"

Pube thought for a minute before responding. "Look, dude, you don't need to worry. It's going to be a minute before you're grown. Besides, I've seen your dad, and he's got big hands so you're going to be fine."

Preeb sighed loudly. "Oh, that's right. I heard something about, it's the size of your hands! But I also heard it's about the size of your feet? So, which is it?"

The audience became animated as they picked up the debate.

Dr. Richard laughed, shouting, "Woah, woah, woah! I've got to stop this nonsense right now." He waited for the din in the room to die down. "I've actually heard grown women talking about the size of a man's hands and feet. I'm not sure how that rumor started," he said, "but we need to put a stop to that nonsense right now. There's no relationship between the shape and size of a man's hands, feet, or any other part of the male anatomy that relates to penis size. I repeat *no* relationship," he said louder for emphasis.

"Penis size can be determined by a number of variables. The primary variables are the genes you got from your parents. They are your best indicator of your adult penis size," he stated emphati‐ 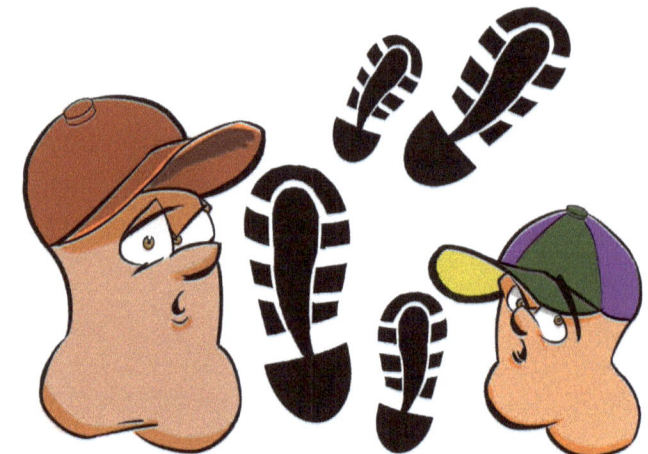 cally. "But it can also be affected by other outside factors, like hormone exposure. While at this time there are no hormones that seem to increase length, exposure to certain hormones, such as environmental estrogens or being exposed to contaminants when beginning puberty, have been associated with shorter penises."

He looked at the audience and saw their expectant faces, so he continued. "Moms being malnourished while pregnant as well as a male malnourished in his early years can also lead to shorter penises. The hormones that drive penis length and width are testosterone and human growth hormone, or HGH." Dr. Richard paused as the audience began animated conversations amongst themselves.

"Now, I don't want anyone running out of the room for hormone injections or HGH pills. Hormone shots have not been shown to reliably enhance growth other than in cases of pre-pubescent boys with a growth hormone deficiency or pituitary problems. If someone is offering you supplements that promise penis growth or enlargement, it's phony. Taking HGH when you're healthy or not under a doctor's care will have side effects." Dr. Richard waited for the audience to quiet down and focus once again.

"Now, since males get a great deal of their self-image from how they feel about their penis size, I want to spend a minute on this topic. I know statistics can be boring, but since numbers don't lie, and this is the best way to prove what I'm saying, I need to share some facts."

Dr. Richard changed the slide on the screen. "Reports show that only 55% of men are happy with their penis size, even though studies have found that **90% of adult male penises are within one inch of the average size**." He emphasized this point for the audience. "So why all the negativity? Because males tend to mis-judge the size of their penis relative to others." Realizing he had everyone's attention, he continued.

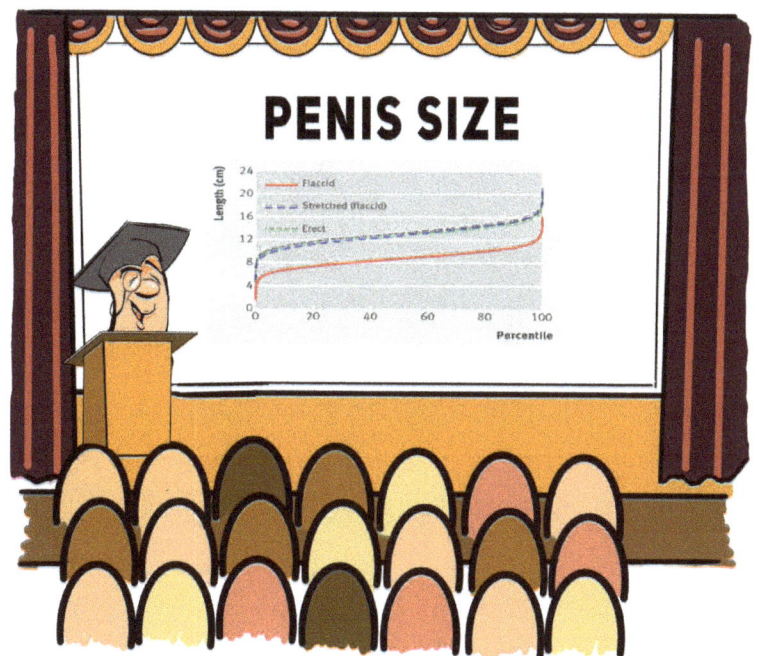

"The most common way a male sees another male's penis is at the urinals. Standing next to someone in a urinal automatically puts you at a disadvantage because of the angle. Looking down on the person next to you will always make them look larger, because of the angle." Dr. Richard paused to let that fact sink in. "The best way to examine your length is to have a mirror to the side of you. In addition, if you see published photos or videos of males, they will tend *not* to represent the general population. They misrepresent what is normal since those individuals are chosen *because* they exceed the normal range."

Dr. Richard paused again, so that he could drive home his most important point. "So, guys, the statistics show you have a 90% chance of being normal. This might lead you to ask, 'Why haven't you mentioned the normal range yet?'" he said. "Because you would stop listening and run to the men's room with a ruler."

The room erupted in laughter.

"So here it goes," he said. "The average size of a *flaccid* or limp penis is between 3.4 and 3.7 inches in length; the average size of an erect penis is 5.1 and 5.7 inches, with a *circumference,* or the distance around, between 3.5 and 3.9 inches."

Dr. Richard smiled at the audience. "Now before you run off to measure, let me tell you how to do it." He paused to make sure everyone was once again focused. "You would measure from the pubic bone to the tip of the glans, and you measure along the topside of the penis. You must press down through any fat until you feel the pubic bone. You must also not count the length of foreskin."

He looked at the group and smiled knowingly. "This is a good place to stop for now. Hopefully this whole discussion has made you feel more comfortable about the growth of your penis."

CHAPTER 17

GROWERS AND SHOWERS —
Can one penis shrink more than others?

The Boyz stood off to the side, half-watching a peewee softball game.

Pube looked at Preeb. "So, you know I'm friends with Peter, right?" he asked. "I thought I should give him a heads up about what they wrote about him on that bathroom wall. You know, the stuff you told me about the other day."

Pube paused as he waited for Preeb to remember.

"He said he's not worried about it because he's a grower. So, those who need to know, will know, and those who don't need to know, don't matter."

Preeb looked back at him, confused. "I'm not sure what any of that means...but okay. So long as he's good. What's a grower?"

"That's a guy whose dick gets a lot bigger when he's excited and shrinks a lot when he's not," Pube said.

Preeb thought about this for a minute before responding. "When will I know if I'm a grower?"

Pube looked at him and said, "You won't know for sure until you're grown."

Dr. Richard clicked off the presentation and turned to face the audience.

"Let's first begin with the understanding that the growers and showers concept is not a scientific thing. The discussion of being a grower or shower commonly refers to whether a smaller *flaccid,* or limp, penis grows significantly when *erect,* or excited. That's what males like to refer to as a grower. Men who do not grow significantly when erect or excited and appear larger in their *flaccid* state are considered showers." He gave the room a moment to digest this information.

"The concept of growers and showers is based primarily on how males describe themselves. The science *does* support that males have differing levels of *elasticity* in their penises. In other words, when *flaccid,* or soft, some men can stretch their penises farther than others. So how would you know whether you're a  grower or shower? A relevant study on this topic defined it this way. A penis that changed from *flaccid,* or soft, to erect greater than four centimeters or 1.57 inches is a *grower*. If the change is less than 4 centimeters or 1.57 inches, it is a *shower*. This applies to a mature penis, not one Preeb's age."

Dr. Richard gave the audience a minute before continuing. "When it comes to this whole issue of *growers* and *showers*, our friend Preeb is at a disadvantage if he starts thinking about it now. Only because he is at an early stage of puberty. He may have friends who started puberty earlier than him, so if he's hitting the showers, he may think he's small in comparison to his peers. The only fair comparison would be against a kid who started puberty about the same time he did."

Dr. Richard continued. "Even though you will not hear guys talking about looking at other guys because it may sound creepy, peeking at the guy next to you at the urinal, in the shower, or in the locker room, happens—and because we don't talk about it, a lot of us come to the wrong conclusion about how we compare." Dr. Richard looked around the room, repeating the fact that, "We don't realize the angle will make us look smaller by comparison, and so some guys will conclude they come up 'short.' This misguided belief can follow them into adulthood and helps us understand why 45% of males are unhappy with the size of their penis when only 5% fall below the normal range. Clearly this is a big deal for guys, and they should be able to talk about it.

"To wrap up, the appearance of the penis is primarily genetically determined. I have an interesting speculation I can share when it comes to the elasticity discussion, better known as the growers vs. showers," Dr. Richard said. "A possible theory is that it is a trait, which developed as a result of the temperature requirements for the production of sperm." He paused, then added, "If you realize that sperm needs to be maintained slightly cooler than body temperature, it is feasible that those continuously exposed to colder climates would need greater elasticity to retract both the penis and the scrotum closer to the body—otherwise known as growers. And those from warm climates may have benefited from the additional coolness of having the penis remain elongated farther away from the body—otherwise known as showers.

"Surprisingly, given the amount of interest in the topic,

there's not a lot of reliable research on the topic of growers and showers," Dr. Richard concluded. "What is clear is that, while there are size variations amongst penises, contrary to popular belief, they occur within a narrow range—especially when erect or aroused."

CHAPTER 18

CURVE-A-HEAD — Help! My penis is curving!

"I was scrolling through this website, and it freaked me out!" Pube said. "It was talking about penises curving being some kind of disease. My dick is starting to curve a little! What do I do?"

Preeb looked sadly at his friend. "Man, I don't know what to tell you...." His voice trailed off.

Dr. Richard stepped forward. "More than likely, what our young friend was reading about was Peyronie's disease. It's really not likely that he has Peyronie's disease. Peyronie's normally affects men between 40 and 70 years of age. However, what Pube is experiencing is quite normal. The reality is, a little bit of *curvature* in a penis during puberty is normal. It should not cause you any discomfort or difficulties.

"So, what's normal?" asked Dr. Richard, looking at the group. After a brief pause, he said, "I really hate to say *normal*. I prefer to say, what's more likely? Sorry to bring out the statistics again, but it's the easiest way to make the point."

Dr. Richard turned towards the screen and the stats depicted there. "As we can see, roughly 50% of males report their erect penises as straight. Another 30% report that their penises veer towards the left, and roughly 6% said they pointed to the right. In addition to direction, the angle of the penis, when erect, can be different as well."

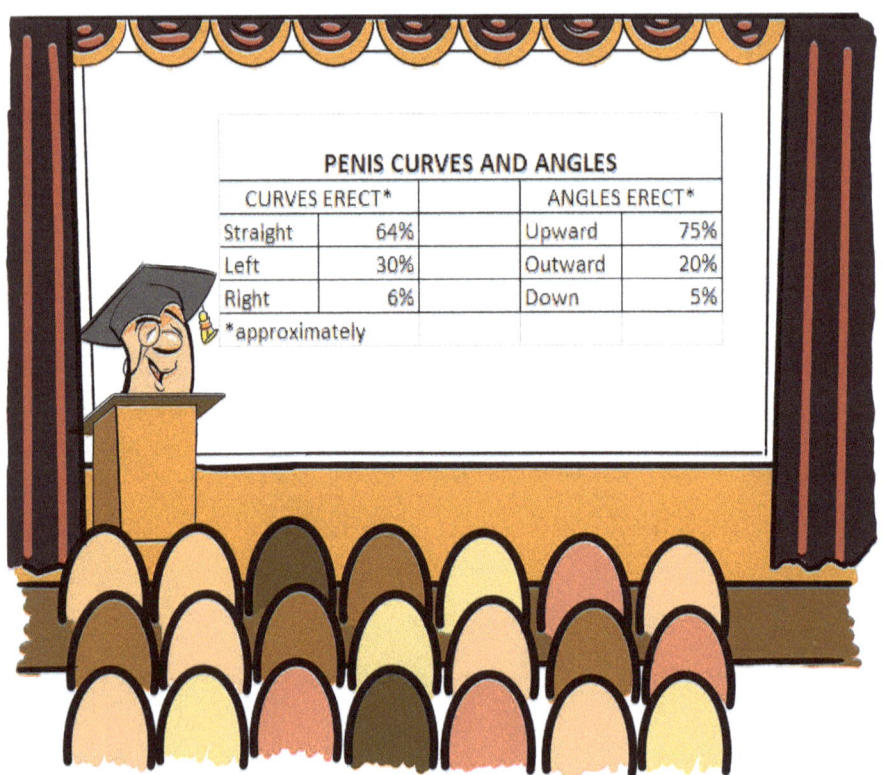

Dr. Richard added, "The majority of males reported that their penises, when erect, pointed upward. Another 20% report that their penises point outward, and 5% report their erect penises point downward. So, when should you become concerned?" Dr. Richard asked. "If you experience discomfort, or you have a greater than 30-degree curve, you should contact a urologist. If it's a slight curve, that's normal. A word of caution: Do not hang weights on your penis in order to lengthen or try to forcibly bend it. You can cause yourself serious injury."

CHAPTER 19

JERKING OFF / JACKING OFF / WHACKING OFF / BEAT THE MEAT / CHOKE THE CHICKEN / SPANK THE MONKEY / STRANGLE THE SNAKE — The truth about masturbation

Preeb and Pube were hanging out in the back yard of Pube's house.

"You would not believe what happened last night," Pube said, red-faced. "It was so embarrassing. After school yesterday, I was in my room choking the chicken, and I forgot to lock the door. My grandmother comes barging in with the laundry. She knocked but didn't wait for me to say 'come in.' She starts freaking out, drops the laundry, and runs out screaming about how I'm going to go blind! I had to skip dinner. I said I was feeling bad. I didn't want to run into her...."

Preeb looked at his friend, concerned. "Do you think she's right about the going blind thing?"

Dr. Richard stopped the presentation and cleared his throat. "Okay, everyone, this is one of those topics that has a ton of bad information still circulating, even though we should know better.

"First of all, since there's a lot of nicknames for this, the correct term is *masturbation*. Simply put, masturbation for males is rubbing or touching your penis to feel good," he said. "Masturbation is a common and normal part of the male experience. Again, I call your attention to the statistics. Between 72 and 84 percent of adult males masturbate at least once a month. Masturbation does not have a negative physical consequence. In other words, masturbation doesn't physically hurt you, unless you grip yourself too tightly."

Turning to the audience, Dr. Richard said, "Let's look at the myths that people are still repeating. These myths have all been proven false. He pointed to a list that appeared on the screen and read as follows:

"Masturbation does not

1. give you hairy palms,
2. make you go blind,
3. give you acne,
4. make your penis shrink,
5. make you go insane or cause any mental illness,
6. cause cancer,
7. make you sterile,
8. give you a low sperm count,
9. interfere with your ability to get an erection now or when you get older,
10. cause your penis to curve,
11. lead you to kinkiness or perversion,
12. give you an STI,
13. mean self-abuse,

14. cause physical weakness,
15. lead to homosexuality,
16. hinder your social and emotional development, or
17. make you unfaithful."

Dr. Richard took a moment to catch his breath before continuing. "Masturbation is only a problem if it interferes with you spending time with your friends and family, and if it gets in the way of you participating in social or athletic activities. If this is the case, you should get advice from your doctor."

CHAPTER 20

NIP - SLIP — Am I getting boobs?

I can't talk to anybody about this, Pube thought, as he looked at himself in the mirror. *I can't be growing boobs! How do I make this stop! They're going to roast me big time. I don't know what to do.* His mind was racing, and he was plenty scared.

Dr. Richard paused the projector. "Obviously, our friend Pube is so disturbed by this latest development that he can't even share it with his friend, Preeb," he said, sympathetically.

Shaking his head, he continued. "Believe it or not, what Pube is experiencing is not unusual. I know a lot of you here went through the same thing. When it happens, some boys are scared they are growing breasts. Others think they may have breast cancer. A lot of boys are scared to tell anyone and suffer in silence, waiting to see what happens.

"This common development causes unnecessary stress and worry," Dr. Richard stated. "All boys have some breast tissue located under their nipples. Changing hormones in puberty can cause the breast tissue to swell. In about 65% of boys, they can develop lumps or feel sore or tender around their nipples.

"Boys can develop more breast tissue during puberty, which can make them think their breasts are growing. The amount of breast tissue is very small. If the developing breast tissue is large enough to be seen, it is called *gynaecomastia*. This condition is also common and does not cause any health concerns.

"In the beginning of this series, we talked about hormones starting production in puberty, remember?" Dr. Richard paused to see whether the audience was following him. "In addition to the male hormones, boys also have some *estrogens,* or female hormones. As the body starts production of hormones, the hormones need a little time to level off—similar to the movement of a swinging pendulum until it settles. This process can take 6–18 months. The breast tissue and swelling should be gone by around age 20 if not sooner," he said. "More than half of all boys experience an increase in breast tissue, so you are not alone. Undershirts and compression shirts under your clothing can help minimize visibility."

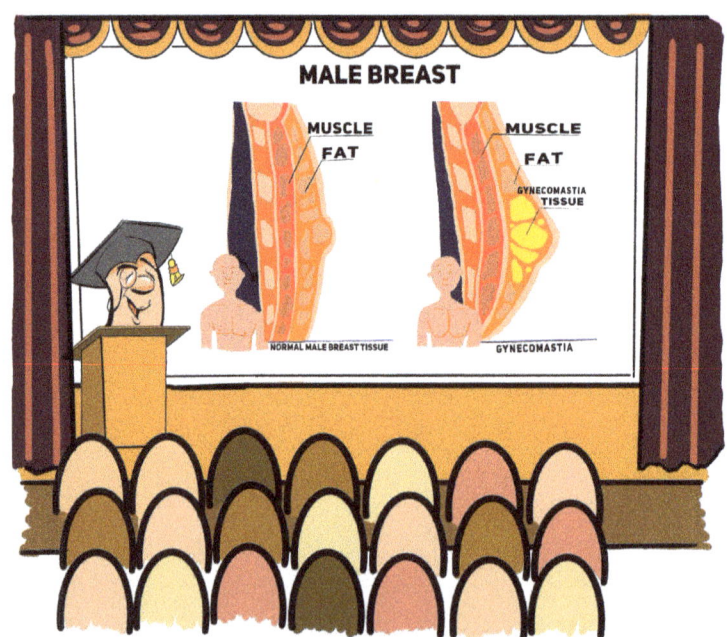

Dr. Richard continued, in a comforting tone. "It is normal for the breast tissue to feel like a lump but know that while it is important to be watchful, breast cancer is extremely rare in children.

"At this point, I need to share some information." Looking back out at his audience, he said, "On a different, but similar note, if you are overweight, you can have some fat beneath the skin of your breasts. This is different from the breast tissue we have been discussing. This layer of fat beneath the breasts will only go away if you lose the excess weight. Hopefully, this information will give our friend Pube some relief."

CHAPTER 21

"LUKE, I AM YOUR FATHER" —
Oil that squeaky voice

Preeb and Pube met by the front gate of the school to head home. Pube looked angry but stayed silent. Preeb looked at him, concerned. "So, what's up, dude? You look really pissed!"

"I got detention tomorrow," Pube said.

"YOU, got detention!" Preeb responded, shocked. "How the heck did that happen?"

"I was in Ms. Lambert's class, and she called on me. When I went to answer, my voice did some funky thing, and the kids started to laugh," Pube said.

"That shouldn't get YOU detention," Preeb pointed out.

"Nah, I got detention because I told Anthony to shut up before I knocked him out! He took it too far! He was making squawking noises, saying I sounded like a chicken," Pube said, angry.

Preeb looked at him, concerned. "Just shake it off...."

Dr. Richard approached the podium after pausing the video. He cleared his throat and said, "Some of us remember quite well what Pube is experiencing. I remember when my voice started to change. I was trying to ask this really cute girl to the eighth-grade dance. I opened my mouth, and this weird sound came out..." His voice trailed off as he reminisced. "Anyway, you're not here to hear about my puberty stories. So, what is going on with our friend, Pube? That special sauce testosterone is at it again."

Dr. Richard pulled up a slide, which showed the inner workings of a young man's throat. "We each have a voice box, called a *larynx*. In the larynx are *vocal cords,* or *folds,* which vibrate when we speak or sing. That vibration controls the pitch of our voice. During puberty, testosterone makes the cords, or folds, longer and thicker. The folds grow almost twice as fast for boys as they do for girls. The change in tone can happen differently. For some, the changes can happen seemingly overnight; for others, it can appear gradually. For most, the cracking will only last about three to four months."

Dr. Richard stopped for a sip of water before continuing. "The change in the vocal cords, or folds, can occur at different times, but on average they will begin to change around age 12 or 13 and should finish somewhere between ages 15 and 18."

Dr. Richard smiled. "There is good news for our friend, Pube. The voice changing has been shown to come right before a growth spurt, so our friend can look forward to getting bigger soon!" Dr. Richard gazed out over the audience and smiled. "Just making sure we have reasonable expectations. The growth spurt will not happen overnight but over the next two to three years."

Dr. Richard thought for a moment before saying, "Now might be a good time to discuss the Adam's apple...and why girls don't have one. If I can have you once again look at the diagram." He paused as the audience shifted their attention. "As I mentioned, the length of the vocal cords, or folds, is longer and thicker in boys than in girls. Consequently, as the voice box or larynx gets bigger, it tilts to a different angle. It sticks out through the neck and becomes visible. This is the Adam's apple." Dr. Richard looked amused as he said, "Mystery solved!"

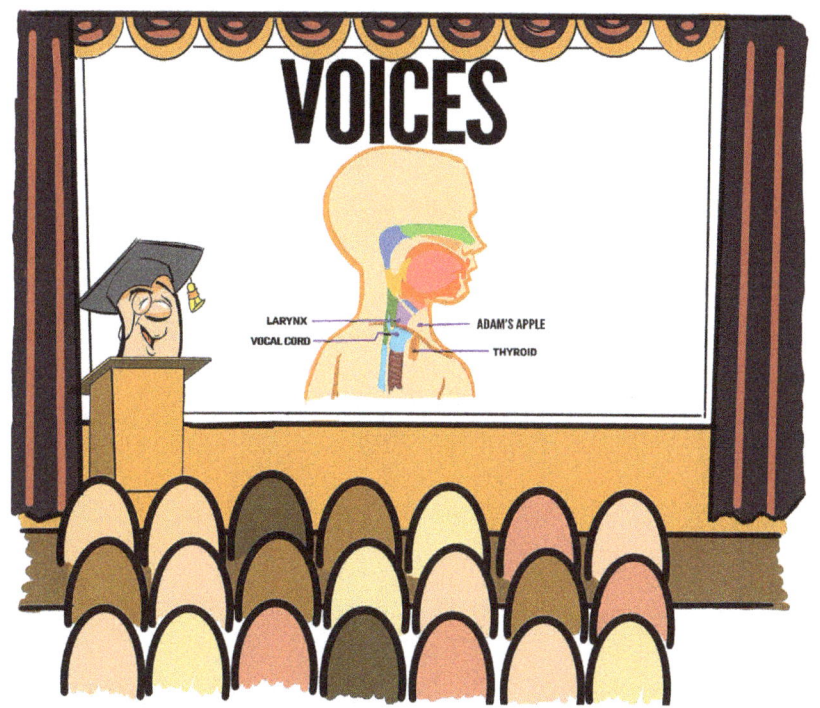

CHAPTER 22

WHY IS EVERYONE IN MY BUSINESS? — Mood swings

As Pube exited the classroom behind a guy with a cast on his hand, Preeb walked up to him and said, "Wasn't that your quarterback, Jace? I didn't know he got hurt during the game. How'd I miss that?"

"He didn't hurt it playing football," Pube responded. "He's telling everyone he fell off a hoverboard, but he told me the real story. He got mad at his parents and punched the wall in his room. Broke a couple of bones in his throwing hand."

"That was stupid," Preeb said.

Pube looked at him intently. "Not really. I kind of get it. Lately, some people have been pushing my buttons, and I get really mad and then sad—like the day my voice cracked in class."

"Or like the day we watched *Guardians of the Galaxy 2.* Remember how you cried at Yondu's funeral?" Preeb asked.

"I thought I told you never to bring that up again!" Pube said, chastising his friend.

Dr. Richard turned to face the audience. "This is one topic that doesn't come up a lot, but everyone here should relate," he said. "As the body tries to regulate the sex hormones, the fluctuations cause an increase in mood swings. A lot of attention is given to this experience for girls going through puberty, but other than the increased anger, it's virtually ignored with boys. This is a major disservice, as males most definitely experience mood swings. A common experience with boys, for example, is they will come home from school and tell you their best friend is really annoying, and they can't stand them, and an hour later tell you the two of them are going to hang out together."

Dr. Richard paused, considering how he wanted to make his next point. "As our friend, Pube, is beginning to realize, boys will be angry, irritable, short-tempered, and sad at times as they go through puberty. They will be confused about why whatever occurred bothered them so much. They will want to yell, cry, punch, feel anxious, get a hug, and they will be confused by their own behavior.

"It's our job to help them understand this *before* it happens, remind them of it *when* it happens, and teach them how to make it right *after* it happens." Dr. Richard stressed his next point. "It is important that we do not meet anger with anger. It's pointless and only makes a bad situation worse. This does not mean that boys shouldn't expect consequences for negative or inappropriate behavior. We *all* need to be aware that actions have consequences. It is, however, an extremely important time for young men to learn how to cope with their anger and irritability. So, how do we help them handle their emotions?" Dr. Richard asked.

"Tell them *beforehand* that they are going to experience mood swings. It's happening because their hormone levels, especially testosterone, are fluctuating. Eventually, it will level off.

"In the meantime, they are still *responsible* for how they act, so they should have a plan. They need to remember to breathe. When we're angry, our fight or flight response sends oxygen away from our brain to our muscles, so the brain doesn't have time to tell us that what we're about to do is a bad idea. I bet Pube's friend really regretted hitting the wall. It probably caused him to miss the rest of his football season."

Dr. Richard paused briefly before continuing. "Getting back to the point. If you take three really deep breaths before doing or saying anything, it will calm you down. Taking sips of water can also accomplish the same thing, so carry a water bottle. If you can't remember to breathe, walk away. If it's still important in an hour, then think about what you want to say and then go say it. It's also a good idea to have a trusted friend who can tell you when you're going too far.

"Know that on occasion you will take it too far. When that happens, accept responsibility, and most importantly, apologize and accept that there may be consequences.

"Next, encourage participation in a physical or creative activity. These activities provide a positive outlet for intense emotions but also encourage control," Dr. Richard said.

"While we're on this topic, I want to touch on something that I know was greatly discouraged when I was growing up." His expression was serious as he looked out at the audience. "I used to be punished for crying. I was told that boys, but more importantly, men, don't cry. I was told to 'suck it up.' Now while I'm not saying let's encourage boys to start crying over everything, I *am* saying, let's stop treating crying as if it's the worst thing a boy can do.

"Crying is a great stress reliever. In fact, crying releases another hormone called *oxytocin*, as well as some other chemicals, which help us feel good. These natural chemicals, called *neurotransmitters*, help us release negative feelings and frustrations and reduce pain. That's why a good cry makes us feel better. When we attach negative messages to boys or anyone about crying, we are interfering with the body's natural coping mechanism. Crying is not a weakness; it is a physical way to heal pain—both physical and emotional."

CONCLUSION

"It has been my pleasure to be here with you during this series," Dr. Richard told the audience. "A lot of information was shared, and I hope you found it informative. At this time, I would like to bring out the real stars of this series, Preeb and Pube."

Preeb and Pube walked up on the stage to thunderous applause.

Dr. Richard waited for the applause to die down before saying, "I want to thank you Boyz for your willingness to step up and share your thoughts and experiences with us. It really helped us get a handle on how *you* understand and experience puberty. We can't thank you enough! Neither of you are done yet, so if you, or anyone in the audience, have additional questions, please feel free to visit my website www.RichardNtheBoyz.com. It is my hope that this series has made it easier for you to ask questions. The only bad question is the one you don't ask. Most importantly, please remember *real men talk!"*

With that, Dr. Richard waved goodbye to the audience and escorted Preeb and Pube off the stage.

AFTERWORD

Why would a female be driven to create a series about the male experience? In particular, puberty? I have to confess, as a single mother of two boys, now in their 20s, with no paternal influence when they were growing up, it never occurred to me that they needed *"the talk."* I had grown up with no brothers and a father who had a very *old-world view* of gender roles. So much so, that my sister and I used to tell him he was lucky God hadn't given him any sons because "we probably would have had to kill him" (mostly kidding). I had no frame of reference for raising boys.

When my oldest son was in the fourth grade at a public school, he came home and told me they had showed him, "the movie." I remember getting a phone call from the mother of one of his friends, and we commiserated with each other that the school should have given us a heads up. If I was honest, while my married friend was concerned that her rights as a parent had been usurped, I was more concerned that I really didn't know the practical realities of *how* boys experience puberty. I did do the appropriate thing and asked my son if he had any questions. I was relieved when he said "No." Years later, he confessed that he'd found my textbooks on Human Sexuality and Growth and Development and filled in his own blanks.

By the time my younger son was in middle school, I was working as an Adjunct Professor teaching Human Growth and Development at the college level. The online university I worked for had an assignment where they asked the students to write a script for "*the talk*" they would have with their daughters about puberty, and they further instructed the students to "pretend" if they didn't have a daughter. There was never any mention of a talk for boys. The school catered to a military population, and so my class was predominately male. Sadly, not one student ever asked for an equivalent assignment for boys. This got me thinking....

So, I started talking with my students at my Community College and a clear trend became evident. Few boys, if any, attending my classes had ever been given the opportunity for a "talk" with an adult. The majority of the boys agreed they would have liked a "talk." The most important trend revealed that...whatever they learned, if anything, in their health classes, did little to help with their practical knowledge of how their bodies worked. In addition, they were still functioning based on quite a bit of misinformation from the locker room.

It wasn't just me, or single mothers—our society continues to perpetuate the myth of men as the strong, silent types who shouldn't talk about what they feel and experience. My students taught me that it didn't need to remain so. With humor, they were able to overcome their resistance to an open discussion about the male experience. Hence, the birth of *Richard and the Boyz*.

—Dr. Nadine Pierre-Louis, LMFT

ACKNOWLEDGEMENTS

I want to take this opportunity to acknowledge those special people without whom this book would not have been possible:

Sherry Wilson King, who helped breathe life into this project. She helped make my vision a reality and provided me with the first actual prototype of my Preeb character. She was my editor, my sounding board, and my cheering section. When a third opinion was needed, she was kind enough to rope in her husband, Alan, a truly special man who understands our quirky, unique, and blessed friendship. Sherry commiserated and celebrated with me through each sentence of this journey, from start to finish, with an unwavering commitment and loyalty.

Andre D. Burke, my illustrator – his love of art, and the joy he gets from creating art, made bringing this book to life a pleasurable experience. He has such accommodating spirit that he never lost patience with my constant suggestions.

My sister, Karen Weller, and her husband, Andrew, who have always been a source of constant support and assistance, most especially through my illness, which kept me housebound. Thank you for always being positive and seeing the humor in this endeavor.

My parents, who have passed, Fernand and Martha, who taught us by example not to worry about what people will think as long as we know why we are following a particular path.

My Miami Dade College – Kendall Campus psychology students, who put up with my jokes in our search of Serotonin and learning. The seeds for this book were planted in my quirky brain from those classes.

I would also like to acknowledge my GWS and S&S Groups. They know who they are. These special people gave me the gifts of acceptance, strength, and courage—the tools I needed to take a chance on myself.

www.ingramcontent.com/pod-product-compliance
Lightning Source LLC
Chambersburg PA
CBHW061128070526
44584CB00033B/4257